PAINTING &
DECORATING
BOXES

PHILLIP C. MYER

745.7
M99P
1997

A NOTE ABOUT SAFETY

Due to the toxicity concerns, most art and craft material manufacturers have begun labeling their products with proper health warnings or non-toxic seals. It is always important to read a manufacturer's label when using a product for the first time. Follow any warnings about not using the product when pregnant or contemplating pregnancy, about keeping the product out of reach of children or about incompatible products. Always work in a well-ventilated room when using products with fumes.

The information in this book is presented in good faith, but no warranty is given, nor results guaranteed, nor is freedom from any patent to be inferred. Since we have no control over physical conditions surrounding the application of products, techniques and information herein, the publisher and author disclaim any liability for results.

Painting and Decorating Boxes. Copyright © 1997 by Phillip C. Myer. Manufactured in China. All rights reserved. No part of this book may be reproduced in any form or by any electronic or mechanical means including information storage and retrieval systems without permission in writing from the publisher, except by a reviewer, who may quote brief passages in a review. Published by North Light Books, an imprint of F&W Publications, Inc., 1507 Dana Avenue, Cincinnati, Ohio 45207. (800) 289-0963. First edition.

Other fine North Light Books are available from your local bookstore or direct from the publisher.

01   00   99   98   97   5   4   3   2   1

Library of Congress Cataloging-in-Publication Data

Myer, Phillip C.
    Painting and decorating boxes / Phillip C. Myer.
        p.   cm.
    Includes index.
    ISBN 0-89134-768-2 (pb : alk. paper)
    1. Decoration and ornament. 2. Texture painting. 3. Ornamental boxes.
    I. Title.
TT385.M94   1997
745.7—dc21   96-50004
                                                             CIP

Edited by Julie Wesling Whaley
Production edited by Bob Beckstead
Cover and interior designed by Sandy Kent

North Light Books are available for sales promotions, premiums and fund-raising use. Special editions or book excerpts can also be created to specification. For details contact: Special Sales Manager, F&W Publications, 1507 Dana Avenue, Cincinnati, Ohio 45207.

Dedication

I would like to dedicate this book to my parents,
Carol and Tony Myer,
who have supported my creative endeavors
through the years.

SPECIAL THANKS

As I am finishing my third book for my publisher, North Light Books, I would like to take the time to thank the individuals I have had the pleasure of working with at North Light: David Lewis, editorial director of North Light; Greg Albert, senior editor; Julie Wesling Whaley, editor and Sandy Kent, book designer.

ABOUT THE AUTHOR

Phillip C. Myer has been painting for over twenty-five years. He is the author of *Creative Paint Finishes for the Home* and *Creative Paint Finishes for Furniture* (North Light Books) as well as ten softcover books on tole and decorative painting. A member of the Society of Decorative Painters for over twenty years, Phillip teaches seminars across the United States and at his Atlanta-based studios. Phillip and his business partner, Andy Jones, create custom-painted furniture and interior decorating through their business, PCM Studios.

TABLE OF CONTENTS

INTRODUCTION

*D*ecorating boxes with textures, patina, patterns, faux finishes, graphic designs, fabrics and papers can be a challenging task. Often, you'll begin your project with a plain or very dated-looking box surface and have the creative job to breathe a new life into it. Even simple painted or crafted effects can dramatically change the look of a box. You may be saying, "Why take the time to decorate a box?" But if you think about it, a box can serve a thousand purposes, from organizing a desk top or kitchen counter to storing important papers or memorabilia.

Decorated boxes can be found in just about every decorating style from modern to traditional. They are also found in about every room of the home from the kitchen to the bedroom. Sometimes they are totally utilitarian, while other times they may be designed purely for decoration. Many interior decorators feel that you can never have enough decorated boxes—they are stackable organizers, good gifts and just great accessories.

So pick up a box and some supplies, determine your color scheme and decorating technique, and begin artistically crafting a beautiful new accessory. Box-decorating projects are not time-consuming, so you'll reap the fruit of your labor quickly. They can be ideal half-day or lazy weekend projects. If you need to stop in the middle of the project, a box easily stores away until you have more creative time to spend on it. Enjoy decorating one or many boxes for your home and to give as gifts to family and friends. ❧

Phillip C. Myer

BEFORE YOU BEGIN

You'll need to gather an assortment of tools and materials to decorate the boxes in this book. These basic supplies will build a "creative tool box" to work with.

BEFORE YOU BEGIN

There are a few things to familiarize yourself with before beginning to decorate accessory boxes. Knowledge and organization are the keys to successful results when executing the techniques taught in this book. Take the time to read thoroughly the next few pages to review the general tools used, basic techniques, brushstrokes and brush loading, as well as transfer, preparation, trimming and finishing methods. Although each project in this book is a self-contained unit featuring the necessary supplies and step-by-step illustrations and instructions, the following "foundation" material will get you started down the right road.

PAINTS AND GLAZES

The house paint coating, art material and craft supply industries have begun the strong movement toward developing and manufacturing environmentally friendly, water-based and water-cleanup products. These products are nontoxic, have little to no odor, and clean up easily with soap and water. The projects found in this book are executed mostly with these environmentally friendly products.

Acrylic Paints

To create your own color mixtures in small quantities, a set of artist's grade or student grade acrylic paints in true artist's pigments will prove useful. I've used Prima Acrylics in the following colors to create a good, basic palette: Cadmium Yellow Medium, Cadmium Orange, Cadmium Red Light, bright red, Ultramarine Blue, Alizarin Crimson, Phthalo Green, Leaf Green Light, Leaf Green Dark, Raw Umber, Burnt Sienna, Burnt Umber, Titanium White, Metallic Gold and Mars Black. By combining these basic colors, you can create any color you need.

Latex Base Paints

You'll need to have a selection of base paints (base coats) to provide the foundation for the paint and craft techniques. Following instructions for each technique, you'll use either a flat or semigloss latex base paint. You can have these colors mixed at a hardware store or home improvement center. Today, most house paint departments have the capability to complete computer color matching. They can match any reference material you bring them (fabric, wallpaper or carpet). For the box projects in this book, a quart (1 liter) of base paint will be more than enough. If you would like to purchase less base paint, an arts-and-crafts store can provide 2-ounce (60ml), 8-ounce (250ml) or 16-ounce (500ml) quantities, but you won't be able to receive custom color matches.

Acrylic Glazing Medium

Many of the box projects require the use of a colored glaze. You can create this colored glaze mixture by adding artist's acrylic or latex house paints to a clear glazing medium. You can buy many ready-made clear glazing products on the market, or you can create your own. You want a glaze product that has an open time (working time) sufficient to manipulate the wet glaze and paint in the desired technique. Due to the size of these box projects, you'll require at least fifteen minutes of open time to achieve successful results.

You can make your own clear acrylic glazing medium by mixing water-based polyurethane varnish plus acrylic retarder plus water. Place equal amounts of these three products in a jar and stir thoroughly. You'll use this mixture as the base glazing medium to which artist's acrylic colors or house paints are added to create a transparent color glaze.

Ready-Made Colored Glazes

You can also find a selection of ready-made pretinted colored glazes. These products are ready to use from the jar. I've used Anita's Faux Easy Glazes for many of the colored glazes found in this book. There are twenty-four colors in the collection and these colors can be intermixed to create new custom colors.

MATERIALS
Decoupage Glue and Fabric Stiffening Glue

To complete the gluing steps found in several techniques, a decoupage glue and fabric stiffening glue will be required. A decoupage glue is a white

craft glue with a very thin consistency. A glue that is extremely thick will not work for paper adhesion methods. You can take a white craft glue that is somewhat fluid, and thin it down with additional water to a flowing consistency. A fabric stiffening glue is thin and creamy in consistency and is used for fabric adhesion.

Foil Adhesive

An adhesive designed for the application of foil gilding comes in a water-cleanup form. This glue brushes on the surface in milky, liquid form but sets up clear. It becomes sticky and tacky after a certain time. This provides a base for the foil gilding to adhere to the surface.

Water-Based Varnishes

Water-based polyurethane varnishes are used throughout the techniques found in this book. Polyurethane water-based varnish, such as Anita's, provides better durability, broad open time, and water and alcohol resistance compared to standard acrylic water-based varnishes. You may choose a satin, semigloss or gloss varnish to provide variety to your finished boxes.

Fragile Crackle Varnishes

This two-part product system creates a cracked or crazed pattern over the surface. These are clear varnish-like products that react to themselves and can produce a crackle finish over any type of surface.

Foil Crackle Medium

This glue-like product forces the foil to separate and form a cracked or crazed pattern on the surface.

Spray Finishes

Spray finishes are manufactured in several forms. Today, there are environment-friendly sprays. Spray finishes are available in acrylic-based products for clear, sealing protection or for coloring. Choose satin, semi-gloss or gloss sheen levels to coat the box surface.

BRUSHES

As you build your technique repertoire, you can also build your brush collection. There are several brushes which are considered "workhorse" brushes that are listed in the supplies of just about every technique. These brushes will get used over and over, but if you take care of them, they will last a long time. All brushes listed here are produced by Silver Brush Limited.

Base Coat Bristle Brush

This is a 3-inch (7.6cm) brush made of natural hairs. The brush hairs are cut at a taper angle to form a sharp, chisel edge. This edge allows you to stroke a straight line; control base paint application; work the brush into tight spots; and stroke on a smooth, even base coat.

Glaze Brush

The glaze brush is two-inches (5.1cm) wide and made from soft, natural hairs. This brush is made like the base coat brush with a tapered cut. The natural hairs soak in sufficient amounts of glaze when loading to allow you to stroke a fair amount of colored glaze onto the surface. Synthetic-hair brushes do not allow you this control because the artificial hair cannot drink in moisture.

Varnish Brush

A 1-inch (2.5cm) brush made of natural hair allows you great control when loading on a water-based varnish. The hairs drink in the varnish, then release it when you apply pressure to the brush. This size brush also allows you to get varnish into tight recessed areas.

Flogger Brush

This style brush is made of a combination of natural and synthetic hairs that measure five inches (12.7cm) in length beyond the metal ferrule. This brush produces unique marks in the wet paint glaze. The long hairs can create strie, flogging and dragging techniques.

Blending Softener Brush

This brush is made from soft, natural goat hair. Available in 1-, 2- and 3-inch (2.5cm, 5.1cm and 7.6cm) sizes, it is needed for fine blending techniques. The soft hairs of this style brush allow you to move paint and blend with great ease.

Silver Mop Brush

The mop brush is made of soft, natural hairs. A size no. 14 has the same qualities as the blending softener brush, but enables you to get into specific areas to control the blending techniques.

Golden Natural Flats

You'll need flat brushes in a range of sizes to complete detail work—nos.

8, 12 and 16. These brushes are made from a combination of natural and synthetic hairs. They have sharp, chisel edges to access really specific areas. They can also paint a clean, sharp edge or line on a surface.

Golden Natural Round

A no. 4 round brush is a fine pointed brush needed for detail and cleanup work. Made of natural and synthetic hairs, it will hold a good deal of paint.

Golden Natural Script Liner

A script liner in a no. 1 size will allow crisp line work. A script liner differs from a standard liner brush by the length of its hairs. A script liner brush's hairs are about ½″ to ¾″ (1.3cm to 1.9cm) longer. This extra hair length holds more paint and creates a longer detail line.

Wash Brush

A wide brush in a ¾″ (1.9cm) size. Made of a mixture of natural and synthetic hairs that load and release paints, glazes, glues and mediums in a fluid motion.

Fan Brush

A large no. 20 fan brush is made from coarse hog hair bristles placed in the brush's ferrule in an arc shape.

Foam Brushes

Polyfoam brushes (sponge brushes) in 1-, 2- and 3-inch (2.5cm, 5.1cm and 7.6cm) sizes are ideal for trim and some base coat painting. They can also be used to apply glue. Do not use them for varnish application; a natural-hair varnish brush provides better results.

TOOLS

The following tools are used in various techniques throughout this book.

Refer to the supply list found with each technique to determine what you need.

Tracing Paper

Transparent tracing paper in pad form (12″ × 16″ [30.5cm × 40.6cm]) or roll form (24″ [61cm] long) will be used to trace and draw pattern design.

Palette Knife and Paint Stirs

A palette knife with a long, wide blade is required to mix the paint and glaze mixtures. The blade should also be flexible. Wood paint stirs are needed to mix quarts of paint.

Wax-Coated Palette and Styrofoam Plates

The wax-coated palette (12″ × 16″ [30.5cm × 40.6cm]) and the Styrofoam plates (with no divided sections) will provide you with surfaces to mix small amounts of acrylic/latex paint and acrylic colored glaze.

Metal Rulers

Rulers in 12″ (30.5cm) and 36″ (91.4cm) lengths with a corked backing to raise the edge of your work surface will be used for measuring and for ruling-pen work.

Ruling Pen

A ruling pen can be filled with thin consistency paints to draw on a fine trim or detail line. It has a slot area for filling with paint and a turn screw to adjust line width.

Craft Knife (X-Acto No. 11)

A craft knife with a sharp blade will come in handy for cutting and scoring surfaces.

Brayer

A rubber base brayer can be used to roll over a surface and apply pressure

to smooth out an area. It is very handy for laying down decoupage prints and sections of paper.

Decoupage Scissors

Small scissors with curved and straight blades are required to cut out prints and sections of fabric. They should have sharp blades.

Fabric Scissors

Large, sharp fabric scissors are required to cut fabric panels.

Credit Card

A credit card can be used as a burnishing tool. With its hard plastic edge, it is good for rubbing down the edge of tape when masking out an area to paint, or rubbing foil in place. A tip of a large metal spoon will provide similar results.

Foil

Rolls of foil are available in gold, silver and copper for foil gilding techniques.

Tapes

Several types of tape are required when painting. They should all be repositionable, allowing you to pull up the tape without harming the coating below. Both 3M's White Safe Release Tape and Blue Long Mask Tape provide good results. Easy Mask's Brown Painter's Tape is wider, providing broader coverage and protection. And it has adhesive only along one half of the tape to minimize the risk of pulling up paint when you remove the tape.

Sandpaper

A variety of sandpaper in grades coarse, medium, fine and ultrafine (#400 and #600) will be required to smooth out or distress the surface.

Miscellaneous Items

The following are some standard household and painting workshop tools. Many are tools "that go without mentioning" when referring to basic methods used in this book. For example, if you are using a quart of paint, you'll need something to open it up with—a paint key.

- Paint key
- Dead pen or stylus
- Pencils
- Erasers
- Toothbrush
- Hammer
- Plastic gloves
- Kitchen sponge
- Natural sea sponge
- Cotton rags
- Cheesecloth
- Household plastic wrap
- Bar soap
- Murphy's Oil Soap
- Turpentine
- Acetone
- Paper sacks
- Paper towels
- Facial tissues
- Clear acrylic spray
- Drop cloths
- Sanding block
- Decorating texture paste
- Wood putty
- Spackling compound
- Putty knife
- White stain-blocking primer
- Paste wax
- #0000 steel wool
- Acrylic retarder
- Containers—small and large butter tubs
- Tack rag
- Gray graphite paper
- White transfer paper
- Tin snips
- Awl
- Upholstery tacks
- Aluminum tooling foil

BASICS

There are a few basic principles that apply to most projects you'll be working on when decorating boxes. Read the following information to prepare yourself for the painting adventures that lay ahead.

STAINING

Some of the box projects require staining before decorating and embellishing steps begin. Staining is quite easy to do on an unfinished surface. Dip a cotton rag into a stain or glaze mixture and begin rubbing color on the wood surface in the same direction as the wood grain. Continue to dip the rag into the color and rub into the surface until an even coverage is achieved. For darker staining, brush on stain/glaze with a glaze brush, then wipe off excess with a rag.

PRIMING AND PREPARING

The boxes that will be decorated with paint or covered with paper or fabric require a coat of primer to seal the surface and create a "tooth" for good adhesion. A white, stain-blocking primer, such as KILZ-2, provides a solid foundation to wood and papier-mâché surfaces. Apply one to two coats, lightly sanding when dry.

BASE COATING

An important step in the process of decorating a box will be applying a base paint to the surface. It is critical that this foundation color go on in a smooth fashion. To achieve good, even base coat coverage, follow a few easy tips. Always load the base coat bristle brush with plenty of paint, saturating the bristles with color, then lightly stroke the brush's bristles across the side of the paint container. You only need to coat from the chisel edge of the brush up the bristles about one to two inches.

Once the brush's bristles are loaded with paint, begin stroking color on the surface. Tackle one section of the box at a time. Apply paint into all recessed trim areas first, then proceed to the larger span areas. Always stroke in long, fluid strokes—short, choppy strokes make for a messy looking base coat and can be magnified when decorative treatments are placed over them.

Apply one coat and let it dry thoroughly. Follow the drying schedule found on the paint label. If you do not allow proper curing time, the next coat can sag and cause curtaining.

CLEANING BRUSHES

Once you have invested in good, quality brushes, it's important to take care of them. When you are not going to use a brush for a period of time and it has paint and glaze in it, you should stop and clean it. Water-based products dry fairly rapidly even when mixed with retarders. So when you are done painting a section, place the brush in a container of water, and when done for the day, take your brushes to the sink and wash them thoroughly with soap and water. Murphy's Oil Soap cleans the acrylics and glazes out of your brushes. Rinse the brush and wash a second time to ensure that all traces of color have been removed from the brush's hairs. The hairs of the brush go way down into the metal ferrule, and you want to remove any paint that may be in there. Shake off excess moisture and allow the brush to dry.

If you've allowed acrylic to dry in the brush's hairs, a small amount of acetone will work some or all of the dried acrylic out of the hairs. Note, the acetone may be harmful to certain types of brush hairs.

PAINTING TECHNIQUES
Side Loading

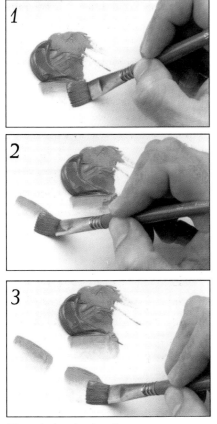

To side load a brush means to carry one color on one half of the brush.

The paint is loaded so that it softly blends away on one side with a crisp line on the other. Dip the brush into the painting medium, blot on a paper towel, and stroke one half of the brush along the pile of paint. Move the brush to a new area on the palette and stroke in short pull strokes, blending the color into the medium until there's no discernible definition of where the color stops and the medium begins.

Double Loading

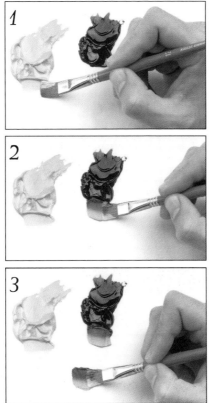

To double load a brush means to carry two colors on the brush side by side, with a smooth blend in between. It's easier to double load a flat brush. Make two piles of paint mixed with medium to a thick, creamy consistency. Flatten the piles with a palette knife to form a clean, low edge to stroke up against.

Begin loading one half of the brush with the lighter color. Stroke both sides of that half of the brush through

the paint. Now stroke the other half of the brush along the darker color.

Move the brush to a new area on the palette. Make short pull strokes to blend the two colors together in the center of the brush. Stroke along each pile of paint again and blend until the brush is saturated.

Pat Blending

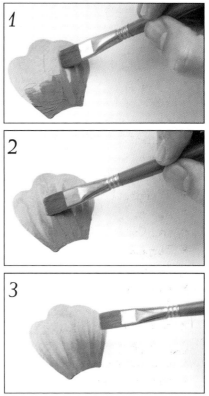

Pat blending softens one color into another, but visible brush marks are left on purpose. Pat blending is used for creating effects such as vein sections on leaves. Place two colors side by side and do some quick brush blending. Now, start at the darkest or lightest point and do a series of pull strokes, one overlapping another to form streaks. The streaks can stay consistent in width or change from small to large or large to small. They can also stay straight or curve to create movement. Continue pat blending from one color into another until you achieve a smooth transition.

Comma Stroke

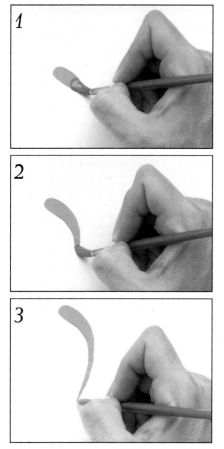

The most recognizable brushstroke is the comma stroke. It is the most important brushstroke to master, for it develops total brush control. Load the brush with paint. Holding the brush at an angle, touch it to the surface and apply pressure to form the head of the stroke. As you begin to release pressure on the brush, curve the brush to the right or left, bringing it up to form a tail to the stroke. When using a round brush, twirl the brush slightly as you lift it up, forming a point with the bristles, which will form the tail of the stroke. When using the flat brush, angle the brush upward, making a chisel edge to form the stroke's tail.

S Stroke

The S stroke forms a shape similar to an S. Load the brush with paint. Holding it at an angle, draw a line.

Curve the brush to the right; apply pressure, dragging the brush to form a pull stroke. Begin to lift up on the pressure, curving to the left to form another line stroke at an angle.

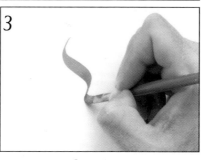

A backwards S stroke can also be completed by reversing the direction of the strokes just described.

U Stroke

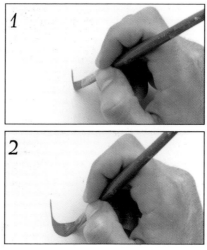

To form the U stroke, load the brush with paint. Stand the brush on its tip and drag it downward to form a line. As you reach the bottom, apply pressure to the brush while curving the brush upward. Pull the brush back up to form a line stroke going upward.

TRACING AND TRANSFERRING

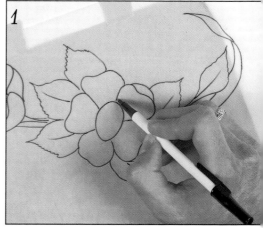

Some of the box projects require the use of a design to follow as guidelines. To use the designs given in this book on pages 104-107 or elsewhere, you'll need to carefully trace the design's basic outline. Place tracing paper over the design and go over the lines with a pencil or fine marker.

Next, tape the traced design in place with several small pieces of tape. Depending on the background color, you'll slip either gray graphite paper (for light backgrounds) or white transfer paper (for dark backgrounds) under the traced design and go over the basic outline. Lift the tracing paper up from time to time to see how well the design is transferring.

TRIMMING WITH RULING PEN

A ruling pen can add a fine line of color to a box to trim out the edge or box top. Thin the desired acrylic color with plenty of water. The paint mixture should be quite fluid but have a little body to it. Load a round brush with thinned paint and stroke alongside the ruling pen's open slot to deposit color. Wipe away excess paint on the sides of the pen. Using a cork-backed, raised ruler (so paint does not seep under), hold the pen at a 45-degree angle and stroke alongside the ruler. Complete all parallel lines first, let them dry and then add perpendicular lines.

FINISHING

After you've decorated the box, you want to protect the finish. Apply at least two coats of a water-based polyurethane varnish over the surface. Use a natural-hair varnish brush to flow on a coat of finish. Always be on the lookout for any varnish runs. Allow each coat to dry thoroughly before applying another coat.

For an elaborate finish, you can apply a series of three coats of varnish, rub with #0000 steel wool, apply three more coats of varnish, rub with steel wool, apply three more coats, rub with steel wool and apply the last coat of varnish. This will provide you with a "glasslike" look.

STONE FINISHING: LAPIS LAZULI

Photo of detail on lapis lazuli box.

apis lazuli is an exotic gemstone of lazurite which exhibits rich, deep tones of blue to azure blue. Due to its color intensity, *faux* lapis lazuli is best when used in small doses. Creating inset panels on surfaces creates a more realistic look when designing with lapis. The mineral is considered a semiprecious stone, so you would not normally see large objects made from it. Metallic Gold accents this stone finish and adds to the exotic and semiprecious feeling. Although it looks elaborate, it is one of the easiest techniques to create. ✤

TOOLS AND MATERIALS

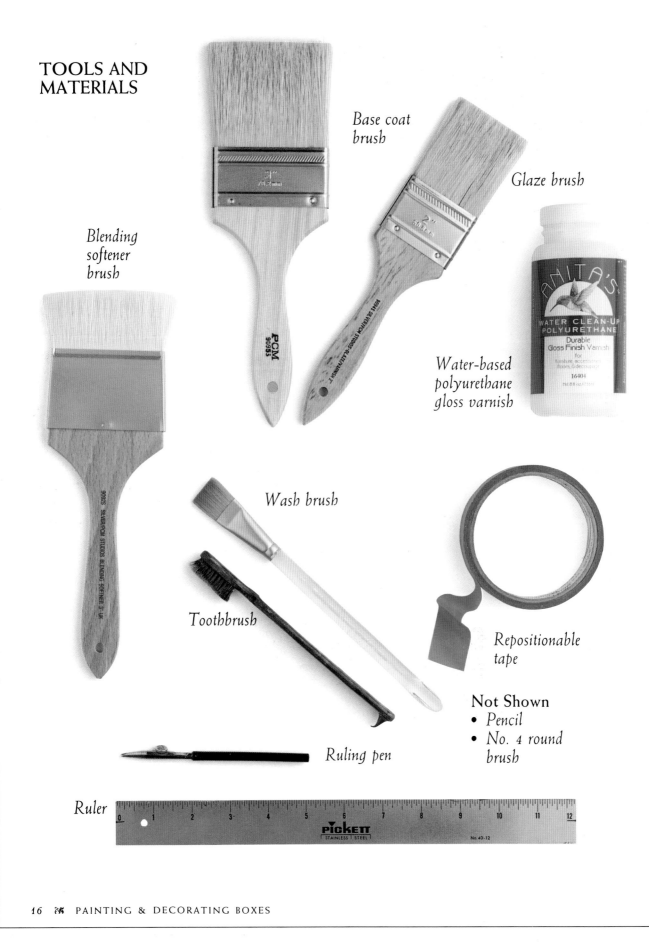

Base coat brush

Glaze brush

Blending softener brush

Water-based polyurethane gloss varnish

Wash brush

Toothbrush

Repositionable tape

Not Shown
- *Pencil*
- *No. 4 round brush*

Ruling pen

Ruler

COLOR CHIPS—ARTIST'S ACRYLICS

Ultramarine Blue
plus black
Ultramarine Blue
Ultramarine Blue
plus black plus
white
Metallic Gold
Dark blue

1 Base coat the entire box in a Metallic Gold acrylic paint using a base coat brush. Apply several coats until opaque coverage is achieved. Measure areas to receive lapis lazuli using the ruler and small pieces of tape for placement. Tape off areas with repositionable tape, rub tape edge with fingernail so paint does not seep under. Base lapis areas with a mixture of Ultramarine Blue plus black using a wash brush.

STONE FINISHING: LAPIS LAZULI

2 Thin all acrylic colors and color mixtures with a blend of 50 percent water and 50 percent water-based gloss varnish to the consistency of a creamy soup. Using a glaze brush, randomly place on color swatches of Ultramarine Blue, Ultramarine Blue plus black, and Ultramarine Blue plus black plus white.

3 Using a blending softener brush in an upright manner, begin blending the color patches together. Lightly dust the surface with the brush in order to mingle colors. Don't apply too much pressure on the brush's hair tips or you will lose color definition.

4 Thin all blue mixtures with additional water to the consistency of ink. Load a toothbrush with Ultramarine Blue plus black and begin flyspecking the surface. Hold the toothbrush firmly in your hand and run your thumb across the bristles while pointing them downward. Repeat with Ultramarine Blue and then with Ultramarine Blue plus black plus white. Let dry.

5 Thin Metallic Gold acrylic with water to the consistency of ink. Using a no. 4 round brush loaded with Metallic Gold, make dashlike marks in a diagonal direction. Feather the gold into the blue background by stroking with a dry round brush. Next, load a toothbrush with thin Metallic Gold and flyspeck over the gold dash-marked areas only. Remove tape and trim with dark blue ruling pen lines.

FABRIC COVERING: IVY PRINTS

Photo of detail on bird's-eye maple box.

Here is a great way to coordinate the fabric elements found in a room (drapes, upholstered furniture, bed linens) with your accessories. This technique shows you how to cover a box with fabric, toning down the fabric through the application of overglazing techniques. This extra glazing step aids in softening the fabric's pattern and coloration. This is a good thing when you are layering a fabric's pattern throughout a room on multiple surfaces. Sometimes, too much of an attractive pattern can visually overpower you. 🐿

FABRIC COVERING: IVY PRINTS

TOOLS AND MATERIALS

Fabric print

Fabric cording

Sponge brush

Glaze brush

Fabric stiffener

Kitchen sponge

Ruler

Cotton rag

Tacky glue

Base coat brush

Scissors— large and small

Brayer

Pencil

COLOR CHIP—LATEX FLAT PAINT

Pure white

1 Base coat in a color to match the background of the fabric. Use a flat sheen latex paint. This coating will create a good ground for the fabric application. A slick, glossy surface would not create strong adhesion and could cause problems. Using a base coat brush, apply a series of smooth coats of paint to the surface. You don't want to create a lot of paint ridges that will telegraph through the fabric once it is glued to the surface. Let base coats dry thoroughly.

2 Take your time and measure ad-joining sections of the box as if they were one piece. You want to create a minimum number of seams. Mark off pieces on fabric with pencil and ruler. Using the large fabric scissors for main cuts and the smaller scissors for fine, curving corners, cut out all pieces. Use sharp scissors to prevent frayed edges.

3 Using a sponge brush, brush a fluid coating of fabric stiffening glue on the back of the fabric and on the box surface. Lay a piece of fabric in place on the box surface and begin smoothing out fabric with the kitchen sponge and brayer. Remove all air bubbles. Be sure that all seam areas and edges are secured in place with glue. Let dry.

4 Thin the base coat paint (that matches the fabric's background) with water to a very transparent, "dirty water" consistency. Using a glaze brush, apply a coating of color to the surface. If the glaze coloration is too transparent, add more paint to the mixture and brush on more. You'll need to scrub color into all the fabric's fibers.

5 Using a soft, cotton rag, begin rubbing the transparent glaze over the surface. First, even out the glaze, and then remove as little or as much of the glaze as you want, to expose the fabric's patterning and color. If you remove too much color, brush on more glaze. Once you are happy with the coloration, let dry overnight. Trim out box edges with a coordinating colored fabric cording. Cut to proper lengths and glue in place with tacky glue.

Woodgraining: Bird's-Eye Maple

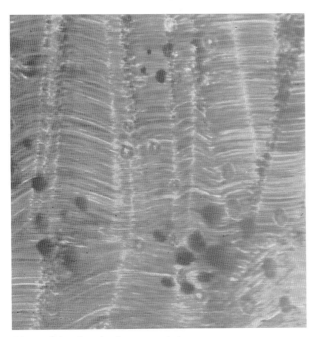

Photo of detail on bird's-eye maple box.

Bird's-eye maple is a rich, amber-colored wood with unusual markings. It gets its name from the dappled patterning with spots that resemble birds' eyes. It is an excellent choice when designing a room or multiple projects with a light colored palette. The golden, yellow tones go well with a variety of colors including rich green, blue and red tones. The wood grain pattern can be made more subtle if you desire by blending longer with the softener brush. Although it has a difficult look, it is quite easy to achieve realistic results. ✍

TOOLS AND MATERIALS

Fan brush

Toothbrush

Blending
softener
brush

Glaze brush

Varnish brush

Base coat
brush and
ecru latex
flat paint

COLOR CHIPS—WATER-BASED GLAZES

Indian Brown

Old Gold plus Indian Brown

1 Base coat the entire box in ecru (a light cream color). Use a base coat brush and apply several smooth coats of paint until an opaque coverage is achieved. Let dry thoroughly before proceeding.

2 Using a glaze brush, apply an even coating of a dark golden glaze (Old Gold plus Indian Brown). Brush long strokes of glaze down the length of the surface. Avoid short, choppy strokes and uneven amounts of glaze on the surface.

3 Using a clean, dry, base coat bristle brush (or glaze brush for smaller areas) and holding it in an upright manner, drag through the wet glaze in short pull strokes. Stop and start the brushstroke movement to achieve these irregular marks. Change the slant and direction of the motion after a few strokes. Once you've stroked from one end to the other, start another row beside it.

4 Holding the blending softener brush in a very upright manner, begin lightly dusting the surface. You want to blur the surface pattern only slightly; don't eradicate it. Hold the brush up in the air and begin sweeping back and forth. Slowly move the brush downward. As soon as you see glaze move, you don't need to apply any more pressure to the surface.

5 To create the bird's-eye patterning, first hit your knuckle into the wet glaze to remove glaze and create light marks. Hit randomly. Next, add dark marks by loading your knuckle with Indian Brown glaze and hitting the surface. Vary the size of the marks, and cluster them together. For additional grain marks, load a fan brush with Indian Brown and add short, curved, dragged marks in the darkest sections. Flyspeck using a toothbrush and brown glaze.

STAMPING: CELESTIAL DESIGNS

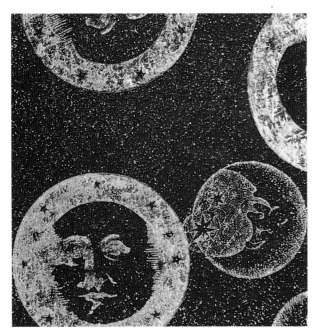

Photo of detail on celestial stamp box.

*S*tamping is one of to-day's most popular crafts. It's an easy technique to execute. Although most people think of stamping on paper surfaces such as stationery, you can stamp on any surface. Wood, papier-mâché, metal and glass surfaces all can be stamped. On slicker surfaces, you just need to be careful of the amount of pressure you apply to the stamp to prevent smearing. Here, sparkling silver stamping is set against a deep midnight blue backdrop. The addition of glitter creates a dazzling result. ❧

TOOLS AND MATERIALS

Stamps—celestial

Stamp pad—silver

Base coat brush

Varnish brush

Clear acrylic spray

Glitter—white, silver and gold

Water-based polyurethane varnish

COLOR CHIPS—LATEX FLAT PAINT
Midnight Blue

1 Clean any dust and debris from papier-mâché box with a damp paper towel. Let dry. Base coat the box with a deep, Midnight Blue tone. Apply several coats until an opaque coverage is achieved. Let each coat thoroughly dry before applying another base coat. Let dry before proceeding to stamping.

STAMPING: CELESTIAL DESIGNS

2 Load the stamp by pressing on the ink pad. You'll need to apply extra pressure when loading the stamp for the first time. Be careful as you start to set the stamp down on the surface and begin applying pressure to make an impression. Movement will cause smearing.

3 Continue to add stamp impressions on the surface. To avoid a rigid, set pattern, place stamp impressions in a casual, random manner. Alternate different diagonal directions for a pleasing look. Be sure to leave some spacing between stamp impressions for smaller stamp designs.

4 Load the smaller stamp with ink. Remember to apply enough pressure when first loading the stamp. Work the smaller stamp in between the larger impressions. Again, be sure to place the impressions on randomly and at various diagonals. A loose, casual look is always more pleasing than a design that is lined up in rows.

5 After stamp designing is completed, you'll need to seal stamp ink. Lightly mist the surface with clear acrylic spray. Let dry. To add glitter, first brush on a generous coating of water-based varnish. While the varnish is still wet, sprinkle glitter over the surface. You can use several types of glitter for variety—white, silver and gold.

MARBLEIZING: GREEN FANTASY

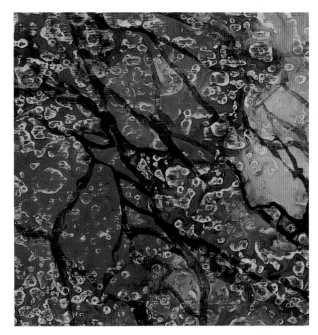

Photo of detail on green, fantasy-style marble.

This painted marble is what is considered a "fantasy style," because it is not meant to duplicate a realistic marble pattern. Basic marble pattern principles have been duplicated but choice of coloration and veining style is more artistic than realistic. You can easily change the coloration of the marble to fit into your room's color scheme. Start out with a light, vibrant base color, then use three distinct hues (vary value and cool and warm tones). The application of the veining is the most critical step, so take your time and be loose. ❦

TOOLS AND MATERIALS

Plastic wrap

No. 1 script liner brush

Toothbrush

Blending softener brush

Mop brush

Glaze brush

No-odor turpentine

Base coat brush

COLOR CHIPS—WATER-BASED GLAZES AND LATEX SEMIGLOSS PAINT

Forest Green glaze

Moss Green glaze

Verdigris glaze

Seafoam latex

1 Base coat the box with a smooth, even application of a light, intense, Seafoam semigloss latex base coat using a base coat bristle brush. Apply several coats until an opaque coverage is achieved. Allow each coat to thoroughly dry before applying another. Three coats should provide enough coverage.

MARBLEIZING: GREEN FANTASY

2 Using a glaze application brush, apply random glaze color patches. Begin by applying a large amount of Forest Green glaze. Stroke on the color in a crisscross style over the entire area. Add patches of Moss Green and then patches of Verdigris glaze. Leave a few openings of the base color showing through.

3 Tear off about a 12" (30.5cm) piece of plastic wrap and loosely wad the plastic into a ball. Begin randomly patting the surface to break up the distinct color patches. As the plastic wrap fills with glaze, pick up a fresh piece of plastic to continue hitting the surface. Your goal is to mingle the colors but not lose the variety of tones.

4 While the glazes are still very wet, load a toothbrush in turpentine and begin flyspecking the surface. As the turpentine hits the wet glaze it will cause a reaction. Small fossilized or craterlike patterns will develop as the turpentine spreads the glaze away exposing some of the base coat color below. Let dry thoroughly.

5 Load a no. 1 script liner brush with Forest Green glaze and begin painting the veins. The most attractive patterning for the veins is a weblike structure that branches out. Place this patterning on at a diagonal to the surface. Once you've painted on an area with veins, lightly dust over the veins with a blending softener brush for larger areas and a mop brush for smaller areas. These blending brushes will slightly blur and soften the veins.

DIMENSIONAL DECORATIVE PAINTING: STRAWBERRIES

Photo of detail on dimensional strawberry box.

*A*dding dimensional qualities to a decorative design provides a tactile experience to the viewer of the work. The subject matter of the design has been built up with texture before the application of color. Since the design is three-dimensional, less time is required in developing dimension through rendering of color and values. Here, strawberries and leaves are rendered, but virtually any subject matter can be developed. Keep in mind that the nature of the texture does not allow for sharp detail. If you desire detail, it should be executed through painting. ✺

TOOLS AND MATERIALS

Decorating texture paste

Palette knife

Mop brush

Toothbrush

Blending softener brush

Glaze brush
Varnish brush

Base coat brush

Cotton rags

COLOR CHIPS—
ARTIST'S ACRYLICS, WATER-BASED GLAZES AND LATEX PAINT

Acrylics—
Alizarin Crimson
plus Burnt
Umber
Bright red
Cadmium Red Light
Cadmium Yellow
Medium

Ultramarine Blue
Phthalo Green plus
Ultramarine
Blue plus black
Phthalo Green
Sand latex base coat

Dark brown glaze
Indian Brown glaze
Black and white
acrylics

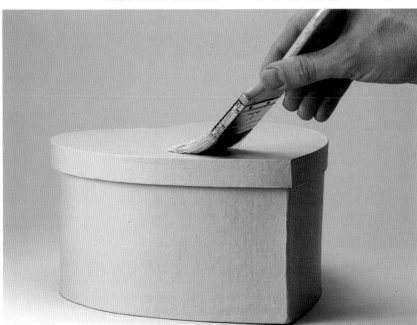

1 Clean any dirt or debris off the papier-mâché box with a paper towel. Base coat the box with several coats of a light, beige-tone Sand latex semigloss paint using the base coat bristle brush. Apply several coats until an opaque coverage is achieved. Allow each coat to dry before applying another.

DIMENSIONAL DECORATIVE PAINTING: STRAWBERRIES

2 Sketch a freehand design, or trace and transfer a design for placement of subject matter. It is not necessary to draw elaborately; simple guidelines are sufficient. Dip the palette knife into texture paste and lay it on within a shape. Scallop the palette knife around the leaf to imitate its shape. Build up dimension in the center of the leaf. If you want them, you can scribe veins in the leaves with the tip of the palette knife.

3 Next, build up the strawberries in a similar fashion as the leaves. Load a sufficient amount of paste on palette knife to develop a "hill" quality to the strawberry. You may need to develop several layers to create a sufficient amount of depth to the center. Let the texture paste dry overnight. Some shrinkage will occur as it dries; if too much occurs, you can layer on more paste and let it dry.

4 You can paint the leaves and strawberries very simply with a "coloring book" approach, or add a little shading. Here, the leaves were painted with the dark green mixture, shaded with black and highlighted with Cadmium Yellow Medium. Base strawberries are in bright red, shaded with Alizarin Crimson plus Burnt Umber and highlighted with Cadmium Yellow Medium. Let painting dry thoroughly before proceeding.

5 Antique the dimensional painting by brushing on a mixture of Indian Brown and dark brown glazes using a glaze application brush. Work glaze into all crevices. Using a soft, cotton rag, wipe away excess glaze. Soften the antiquing by lightly dusting the surface with mop and blending softener brushes. To add extra visual interest, use a toothbrush to flyspeck the background with dark brown.

Paper Covering: Marbleized and Natural

Photo of detail on paper-covered box.

Paper-covered boxes using marbleized and natural papers create the look of a book with handcrafted bookbinding. The finished result has a handsome, tailored look that can be masculine in its appeal. You can develop a feeling of inlaid qualities through the design of panels or insets of various coordinated papers. Any areas that are not covered in paper should receive a coating of a matching paint color to create a unified look. A box is most attractive when decorated with at least three different papers in a similar color scheme. ॐ

TOOLS AND MATERIALS

Kitchen sponge

Decoupage glue

Not Shown
- *Ruling pen (optional)*
- *Base coat brush and white primer*

Pencil

Glaze brush

Brayer

Natural and marbleized papers

Scissors— large and small

Craft knife/ X-Acto knife

Ruler

COLOR CHIPS—LATEX FLAT PAINTS

Greenish gray

Metallic Gold

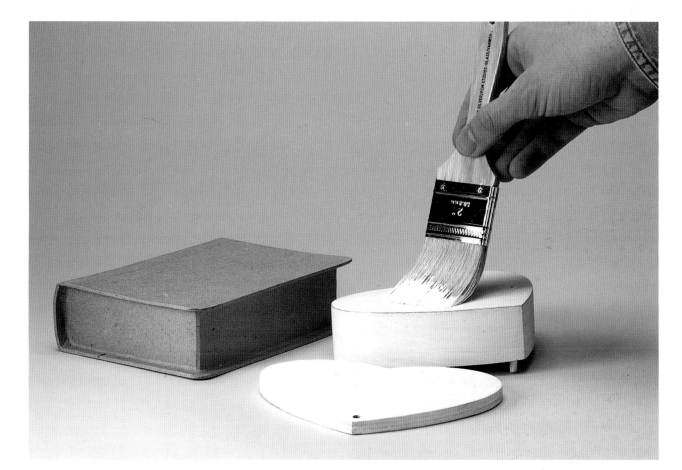

1 Base coat the box of your choice in a white primer. After the primer has dried, coat the box in the deepest shade found in the darkest paper you'll be using to cover. In this sample, a greenish-gray color was chosen. Base coat the box in a flat latex paint. The flat surface will create a "tooth" for the glue and paper to grab hold.

PAPER COVERING: MARBLEIZED AND NATURAL

2 Measure all surfaces of the box to be covered. Determine which paper will provide the background, and measure and mark individual pieces of paper. Cut them out using a ruler and X-Acto knife. Use the scissors to cut out curved or rounded corners and shapes. Place all pieces on the box's surfaces to determine if cuts have been made correctly.

3 Brush a smooth coating of decoupage glue on the back of each piece of paper using a glaze brush or small brush. Quickly place the piece of paper where you wish it to go. Work from the background forward. Lay down the full sheets first and then add inset panels on top.

4 To remove any air bubbles and to squeeze excess glue from underneath the paper, roll over the paper with a rubber brayer. Apply firm pressure to achieve good adhesion between the many layers of the different papers. Always work from the center of the paper outward in a radiating pattern. This will help prevent wrinkles from forming.

5 Remove all traces of glue by wiping the surface with a damp kitchen sponge. Don't apply too much moisture or you can lose the top layer of paper off the surface. The paper may appear "spotty" while sections are wet and drying at different rates. All these should dry out smooth and even. For an optional step, you can add gold ruling pen lines to trim.

DECOUPAGE: FRUIT DESIGNS

Photo of detail on decoupage fruit box.

What makes this decoupage project unique is the application of painted prints. Once the painted, reproduced prints are cut out and adhered to the surface, a hand-painted look is achieved on the box surface. The addition of distressing, crackling and antiquing adds to the illusion—plus provides a very tactile surface. Decoupage is a quick technique for applying a repetitive, decorative design element to a surface. But with today's quality water-based varnishes, it is no longer necessary to build up excessive amounts of finish as was done in decoupage's heyday.

TOOLS AND MATERIALS

Base coat
brush

Sponge brush

Fragile crackle
base and top
varnish

Glaze brush

Decoupage
scissors

Decoupage
glue

Sandpaper—
coarse and
medium-grade

Decoupage
prints

Cheesecloth

COLOR CHIPS—LATEX FLAT PAINTS AND WATER-BASED GLAZES

Leaf Green Dark
 latex
Black glaze
Dark brown glaze
Indian Brown glaze

Black latex

1 Stain the box with Indian Brown glaze. Brush on Indian Brown with a glaze brush and wipe off with cheesecloth. Let dry. Base coat the box with flat latex paint in a dark green tone. Apply several coats until opaque coverage is achieved, using a base coat bristle brush.

2 Using coarse sandpaper, sand through the green base coat to expose the stained wood below. After initial areas are sanded through, switch to a medium grade sandpaper and complete some softer areas of sanding. Dust off the surface.

DECOUPAGE: FRUIT DESIGNS

3 Cut out decoupage prints from printed paper using the small straight or curved decoupage scissors. When cutting paper, always turn the paper into the cut. This will make cleaner, sharper cuts, versus moving the scissors around the paper.

4 Use the sponge brush to apply a sufficient amount of decoupage glue to the back of the cut paper. Apply prints that are to be in the background first, and layer center-of-interest prints last.

5 Quickly lay decoupage print down to adhere to the surface. Work any air bubbles out with your fingertips. Let decoupage prints dry overnight before proceeding.

6 To crackle over decoupage print, apply fragile crackle base varnish using a glaze brush. Let the varnish dry and then apply fragile crackle top varnish. Allow cracks to form during the drying process. Antique the surface with dark brown and black glazes. Brush on the glazes, allowing them to catch in cracks, and wipe off excess. Trim edges with straight black latex paint with a sponge brush.

TIN PIERCING: GRAPHIC DESIGN

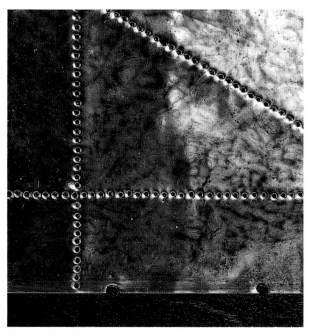

Photo of detail on tin pierced box.

Tin piercing or punching is a very old craft form dating in the United States to the colonial period. Objects such as lanterns, pie safes and candlesticks were made of different metals and then pierced with designs for functional and decorative reasons. Here, a purely decorative approach has been taken with the patterning being updated from colonial designs to a much more modern look. The technique does not require a lot of skill, and although it may look time-consuming, the piercing of a design goes quite fast. Mixing different materials—adding the tin panel to the wood surface—creates a pleasing look. ❧

TOOLS AND
MATERIALS

Toothbrush

Cotton rags

Upholstery
tacks

Tin snips

Awl

Repositionable
tape

Aluminum
tooling
foil

Hammer

No-odor
turpentine

Pattern on paper or
tracing paper

Glaze brush

COLOR CHIPS—ARTIST'S OIL AND WATER-BASED GLAZE

Payne's Gray oil

Black glaze

1 Dip a cotton rag into a water-based black glaze and begin to stain unfinished wood. Rub the glaze, following the direction of the wood grain. Wipe away excess glaze to expose grain markings. You can stain the wood as light or dark as you desire. As the rag becomes saturated with glaze, pick up a fresh rag.

TIN PIERCING: GRAPHIC DESIGN

2 Cut aluminum tooling foil to the desired size with tin snips. Center it on the wood surface and tack it in place using a hammer and upholstery tacks. Place a tack every ½″ (1.3cm), and pierce *through* the foil. It is not sufficient to place the tacks next to the foil with only the tack heads overhanging the foil edge.

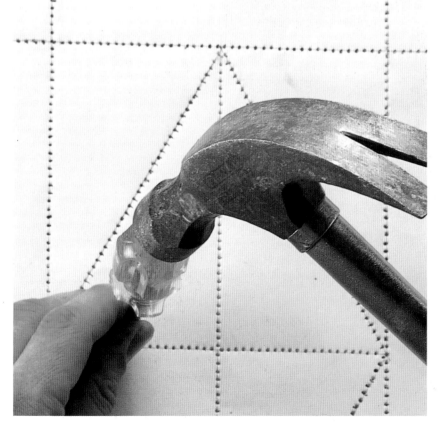

3 Create a pattern on paper or tracing paper. Draw out the lines of the design, then go back and place a dot marking every ¼″ (0.6cm) for piercing points. Tape the pattern in place. Holding the awl in an upright manner over the dot points, tap it with a hammer, using consistent pressure. This will create pierced marks of similar size.

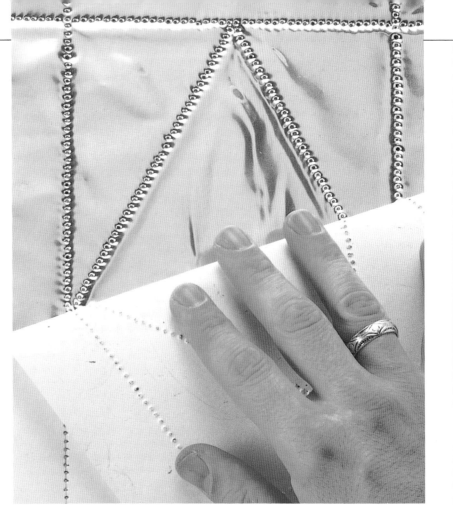

4 You'll need to see how the pattern is reproducing from time to time. Carefully pull the pattern back and check on how consistent the pierce-hole sizes are, and for any missed pierce points. Secure the pattern in place again and continue reproducing the design. After all piercing is complete, pull off the pattern.

5 The aluminum at this point is distracting and shiny. Tone it down through antiquing. Here, Payne's Gray oil paint was thinned down with turpentine and brushed on with a glaze brush. To achieve a pitted look, flyspeck the surface with a toothbrush loaded with turpentine.

LACE STENCILING: ROSE AND LEAVES

The illusion of lace is created on the box surface by stenciling through a decorative paper doily. It's a technique that gives an elegant flair to a box surface very quickly. Spray-paint stenciling was used in this method, but traditional stenciling methods could be employed. It can stand alone or can be used as a backdrop to any decorative painting subject matter. Here, a design of a stroke rose and leaves was added over the lacelike background on the heart-shaped papier-mâché box. This project would make a great Mother's Day gift.

Photo of detail on lace stencil rose box.

TOOLS AND MATERIALS

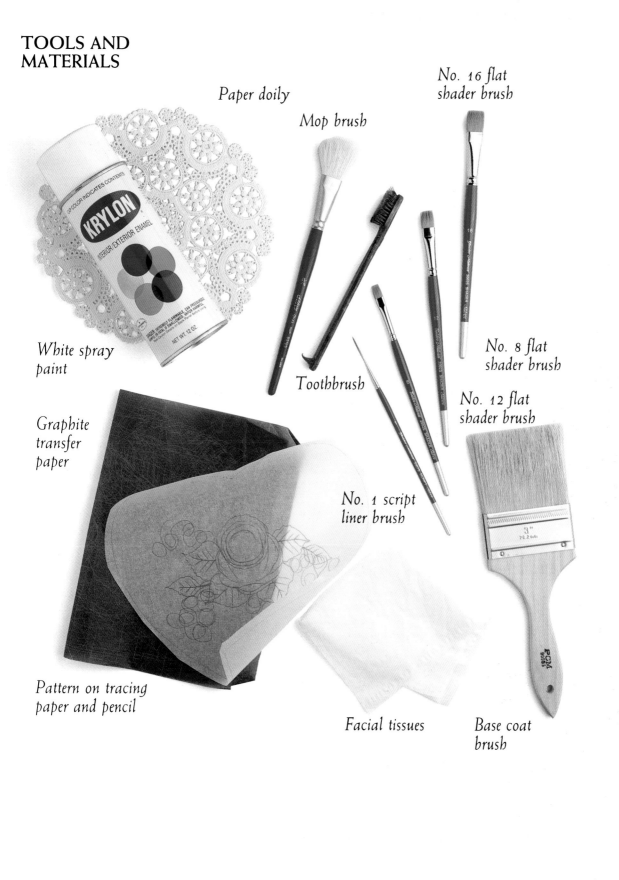

Paper doily

Mop brush

No. 16 flat
shader brush

White spray
paint

Toothbrush

No. 8 flat
shader brush

No. 12 flat
shader brush

Graphite
transfer
paper

No. 1 script
liner brush

Pattern on tracing
paper and pencil

Facial tissues

Base coat
brush

COLOR CHIPS—ARTIST'S ACRYLICS AND WATER-BASED GLAZES

Burnt Umber
Alizarin Crimson
Alizarin Crimson
   plus Burnt
   Umber plus
   Titanium White
Cadmium Yellow
   Medium
Ultramarine Blue
Titanium White
   plus Ultramarine
   Blue plus black
Dark brown glaze
Indian Brown glaze

Phthalo Green plus
   black
Phthalo Green
Mars Black
Titanium White

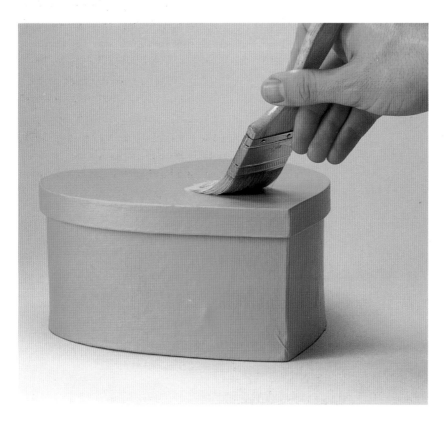

1 Base coat the box in medium value pink mixture (example uses Alizarin Crimson plus Burnt Umber plus Titanium White) using the base coat bristle brush. Apply several coats until an opaque coverage is achieved. Allow each coat to dry thoroughly before applying another coat.

2 Position paper doily where you desire. In a back-and-forth sweeping motion, lightly mist the surface with white spray paint. Work slowly to build up paint coverage. A heavy coating will cause paint to bleed and seep under the paper doily, causing a blurred look to the pattern. Let each coat dry. Lift the doily off the surface once all coats are thoroughly dry.

3 Trace and transfer the pattern using the gray graphite paper. Create interest behind the rose by shading around the design with Burnt Umber. Dip a no. 16 flat shader brush in water and stroke one half of the brush into Burnt Umber. Blend brush on palette and begin stroking next to the design's edge. Feather out color softly by patting with a finger wrapped in facial tissue and blend with a mop brush.

LACE STENCILING: ROSE AND LEAVES

4 Base coat leaves in a mixture of Phthalo Green plus Cadmium Yellow Medium plus black. Shade at the base of each leaf by side loading a no. 12 flat brush with Mars Black. Create two values of a Burnt Pink (light and dark) out of Alizarin Crimson plus Burnt Umber plus Titanium White. Double load a no. 16 flat brush with the dark and light pink mixtures to begin stroking on the rose structure.

5 Highlight the leaves and create veins sections by side loading a no. 8 flat brush with an Ice Blue mixture of Titanium White plus Ultramarine Blue plus black. Stroke on individual veins sections by pat blending out from the center vein. Accent veins with a thin line of Ice Blue using a liner brush. Complete the rose structure with the double load no. 16 flat brush with the two values of pink. Optional background flyspecking in green can be done with a toothbrush. You can lightly antique the box with a mixture of Indian Brown and dark brown glazes if you wish.

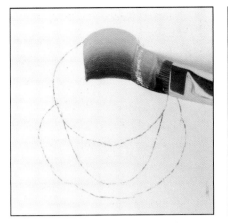

Create a scalloped arc stroke for the back of the rose.

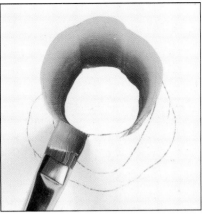

Paint two comma strokes on either side of the arc stroke.

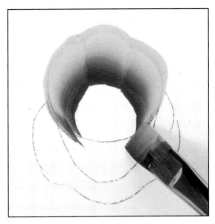

Repeat above steps, stroking on a second layer of petals slightly lower.

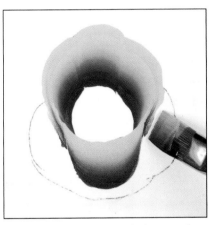

Create the first bowl of the rose by using a U stroke.

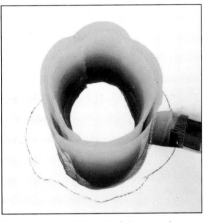

Drop a second bowl of the rose lower, stroking on another U stroke.

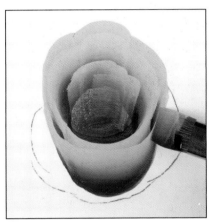

Fill in the throat of the rose by patting the brush upward. Restroke bowl.

Develop side petals by stroking on sliced comma strokes.

Add a lower level of side petals with smaller slicelike comma strokes.

Add a center lower petal by stroking on a "lazy S" stroke.

CRACKLING: FOIL FINISH

Photo of detail on crackled foil box.

The pattern of a dry desert is duplicated over a gold foil for an unusual effect. Finishes that show age and patina have grown in popularity in decorating circles due to their casual and tactile appearances. The cracked pattern is accentuated through the use of antiquing in a dark, transparent earth tone glaze. The glaze collects in the cracks, developing the "dry desert" pattern. The same technique could be executed in a cool color by using a silver foil base and Payne's Gray antiquing.

TOOLS AND MATERIALS

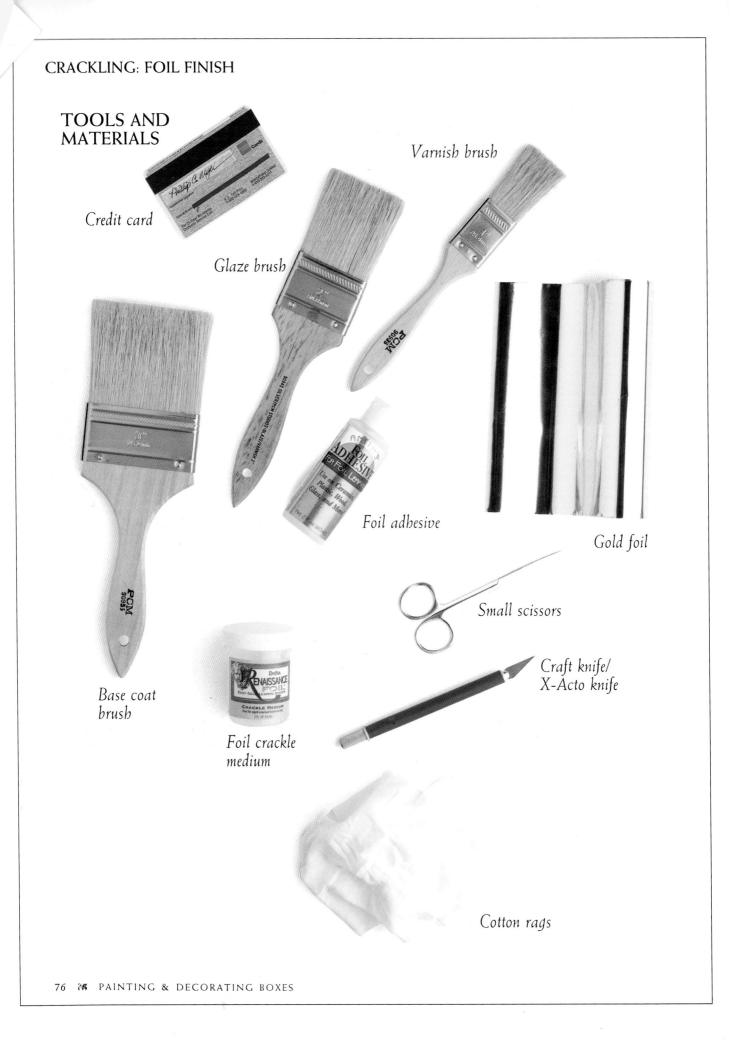

Credit card

Varnish brush

Glaze brush

Base coat brush

Foil adhesive

Gold foil

Small scissors

Craft knife/ X-Acto knife

Foil crackle medium

Cotton rags

COLOR CHIPS—WATER-BASED GLAZES

*Dark brown glaze
and latex paint*

Indian Brown glaze

1 Base coat the box with a dark brown semigloss latex paint. Apply several coats using the base coat bristle brush until an opaque coverage is achieved. Allow each coat to dry thoroughly before applying another. Let the final coat dry before proceeding.

CRACKLING: FOIL FINISH

2 Apply a flowing coat of foil adhesive to the box surface using a small varnish bristle brush. Be sure to achieve full coverage because the gold foil will not adhere to an area of the surface that has not received adhesive. Let the adhesive dry slightly until it turns from a milky white to a clear, shiny coating.

3 Cut foil with scissors or X-Acto knife into manageable pieces approximately 3″ × 5″ (7.6cm × 12.7cm). Lay the foil dull side down over the adhesive and begin burnishing the foil onto the surface with a credit card. Use your thumbnail or the tip of a spoon to reach foil into any crevice area. You don't need to worry about getting full coverage with the foil—leaving areas where the base coat shows through is satisfactory.

4 After the gold foil has been applied to most of the box surface, you can begin the crackling step. Load a small varnish brush with foil crackling medium and begin brushing over the gold foil. Apply a generous amount of crackle medium. As it starts to dry, cracks will begin to form. Let it dry.

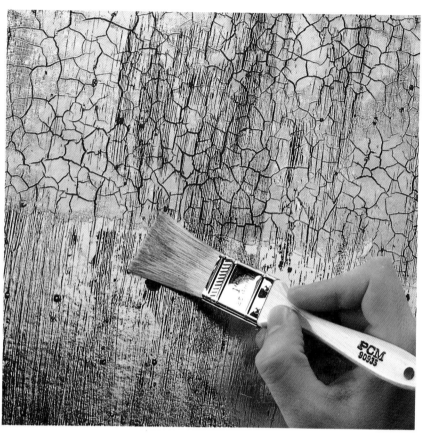

5 Antique the surface with a mixture of dark brown and Indian Brown glazes. Apply a generous amount of the glaze mixture with a glaze brush. Using a cotton rag in a wadded loose-ball form, wipe off excess glaze, allowing it to collect in all the cracks. As the rag collects glaze, discard it and pick up a fresh one.

DESIGN PRESSING: VEGETABLES

Photo of detail on design-pressed vegetable box.

Design pressing is actually a form of stamping a design over a surface in a repetitive fashion. You can take a basic approach where color is simply applied to the press, then transferred to the surface, or you can elaborate on the pressed designs with additional detail painting. The addition of the detail painting provides the finished result with a total hand-painted look in a fraction of the time. Pressing can be done in a loose, *casual method*—a design-as-you-go approach—or a *structured method*—placement of presses laid out in advance. ❧

TOOLS AND MATERIALS

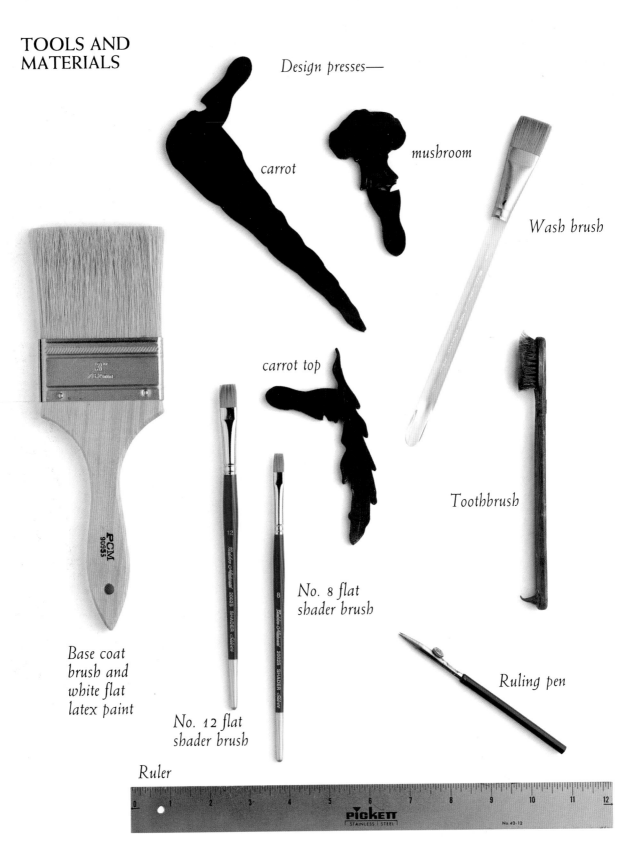

Design presses—

carrot

mushroom

Wash brush

carrot top

Base coat brush and white flat latex paint

No. 12 flat shader brush

No. 8 flat shader brush

Toothbrush

Ruling pen

Ruler

COLOR CHIPS—ARTIST'S ACRYLICS

Bright red
Cadmium Orange
Burnt Sienna
Raw Umber

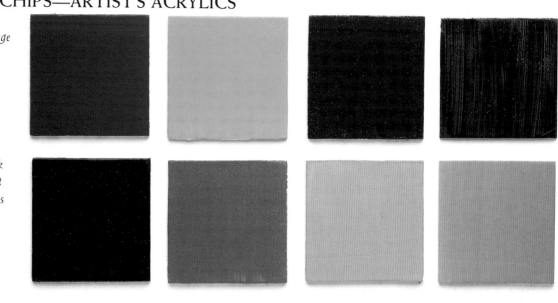

Leaf Green Dark
Leaf Green Light
Raw Umber plus
white
Titanium White

1 Base coat the box with white flat latex paint using the base coat bristle brush. A semigloss surface is too slick and will cause the design impressions to blur slightly. Apply several coats until an opaque coverage is achieved. Let each coat dry thoroughly before applying another.

DESIGN PRESSING: VEGETABLES

2 Thin all acrylic colors that you plan to use for pressing on designs with water to a thin, creamy consistency. Coat the back of the carrot press with Cadmium Orange using a no. 12 flat shader brush. Apply an even coating of color to the press.

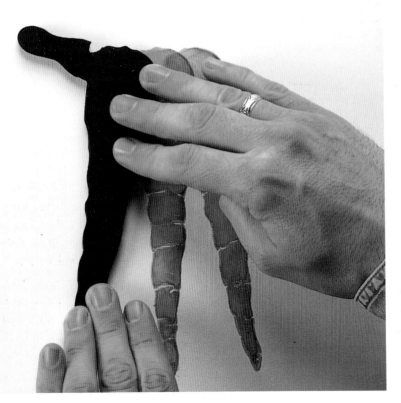

3 Turn the press over and lay it in place carefully. Apply pressure with your fingertips as you make the paint impression of the carrot on the surface. You can lift off the press, reapply paint and make a second impression on top of the last one to deepen color value.

4 To define the presses' images, you can add details with a brush. Side load a flat shader brush with Burnt Sienna and shade down and around the perimeter of the carrot, following the contour and crease pattern that the press has made. Go over the shading with several layers of side-loaded color to build values.

5 Apply carrot tops with the same method, using a combination of Leaf Green Light and Leaf Green Dark. Add detail by side-load shading with Leaf Green Dark on a no. 8 flat shader brush. Mushrooms on the side of the box were executed in a mixture of Titanium White plus Raw Umber, and side-load shaded with Raw Umber using a wash brush. Flyspeck the surface with Raw Umber and add bright red ruling pen line work.

Woodgraining: Mahogany

Photo of detail on mahogany wood-grained box.

Faux bois (French for "false wood") duplicates real wood patterns through the use of tools, brushes and paints. Mahogany is a rich, deep-red toned wood that has an elegant and expensive look. The grain markings are dark, black tones that rest over a luminous reddish background. You can take an inexpensive wood and make it look like it is more expensive mahogany, or take a surface such as papier-mâché and create a wood illusion. The finished effect of *faux* mahogany woodgrain has a very tailored, masculine appeal. ◆

TOOLS AND MATERIALS

Blending softener brush

Natural sea sponge

Glaze brush

Flogger brush

No. 1 script liner brush

Water-based polyurethane semigloss varnish and varnish brush

Base coat brush and Burnt Red flat latex paint

Fan brush

COLOR CHIPS—WATER-BASED GLAZES

Black glaze

Dark brown glaze

Brown Bark glaze

Indian Brown glaze

1 Base coat the box in a Burnt Red (red oxide) flat latex paint. Apply several coats with a base coat bristle brush. Allow each coat to dry thoroughly before applying another coat. Let the last coat dry several hours before proceeding.

WOODGRAINING: MAHOGANY

2 Begin by placing random color patches on the box using a glaze application brush. First, place on a fair amount of Indian Brown glaze, add less of dark brown glaze and Brown Bark glaze, finishing with black glaze color patches. Cover at least 90 percent of the surface with glaze colors.

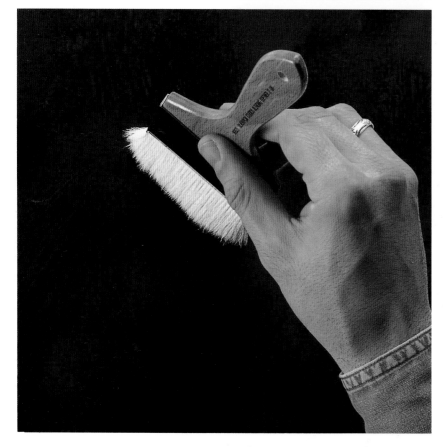

3 Break up color patch divisions by lightly dusting the surface with a blending softener brush. Hold the brush upright and move it back and forth in a sweeping motion. As soon as you see the glaze coloration start to move, do not apply any more pressure on the brush.

4 Using the flogger brush in a hopping motion, begin hitting the surface. The brush motion should be: hit or slap the surface, lift the brush in the air, move slightly and hit the surface again. Repeat this over the entire surface. A fine, dashlike pattern will create an illusion of a grained design. Let it dry and protect it with a coat of varnish. The varnish will allow you to wipe off unsatisfactory grain marks if needed in the next step.

5 To create the dark, long-grained marking, load a fan brush with black glaze. To remove excess glaze on the fan brush, tap the brush's tips on a damp sea sponge. This will result in a brush that is faintly loaded with color. Drag the fan brush down the surface in a linear but slightly wavy pattern. After stroking on a set of marks, brush across the marks with a blending softener brush to blur slightly. Fine, detailed grain markings can be added with a liner brush and black glaze.

MASKING: LEAF MOTIF

Photo of detail on leaf motif masked box.

A graphic approach has been taken with this masking technique. Masking fluid, which, traditionally, is used in watercolor painting, was applied over a base-coated wood surface to protect that area while the background received a golden strie finish. The masked design actually creates a negative space once the dried "rubbery" masking fluid is removed. A simple outlining technique is added to define the graphic, leaf motif in gold. Although there are a few more steps involved with this technique, the finished product evolves quickly. ❧

TOOLS AND
MATERIALS

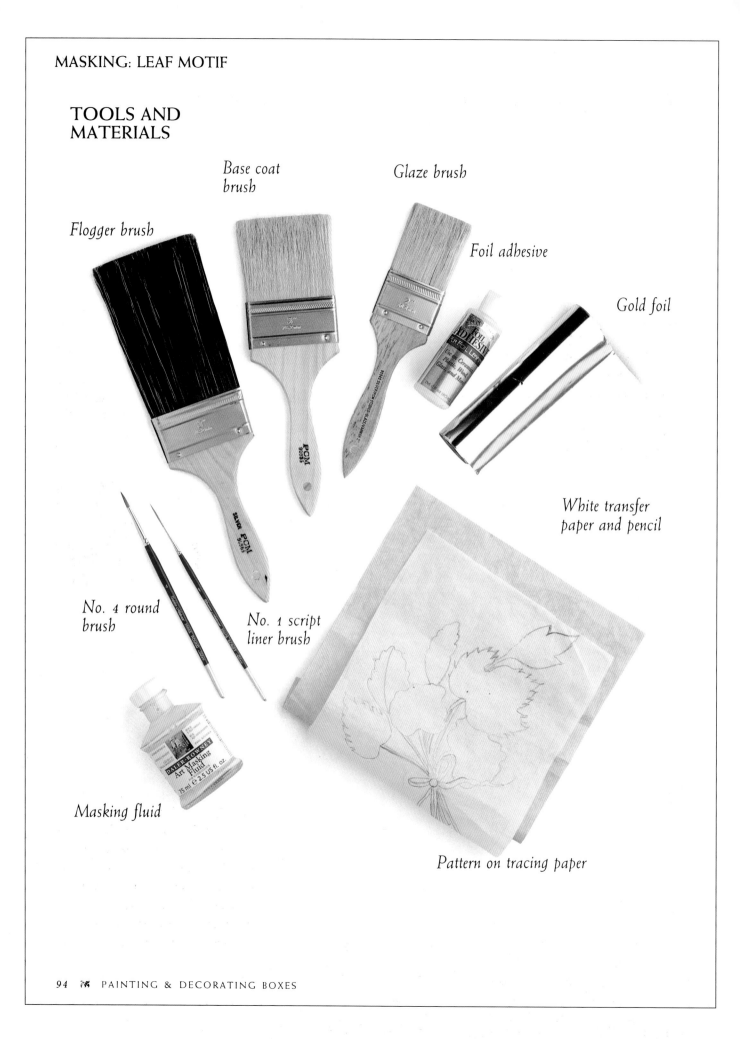

Base coat
brush

Glaze brush

Flogger brush

Foil adhesive

Gold foil

White transfer
paper and pencil

No. 4 round
brush

No. 1 script
liner brush

Masking fluid

Pattern on tracing paper

COLOR CHIPS—LATEX PAINT AND WATER-BASED GLAZE

Leaf Green latex

Metallic Gold glaze

1 Base coat the box with Leaf Green paint using a base coat bristle brush. Apply several coats until an opaque coverage is achieved. Allow each coat to dry thoroughly before applying another. Let the last coat dry several hours before proceeding to the next step.

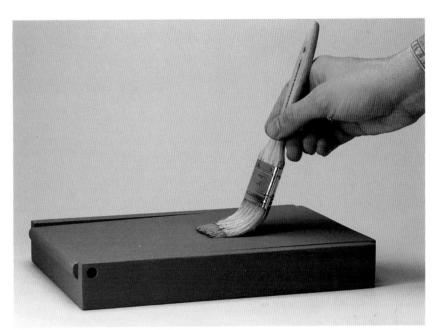

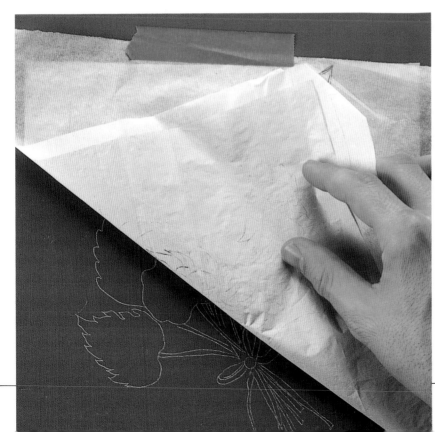

2 Transfer your traced design by slipping white transfer paper right side down underneath the tracing paper and drawing over the design lines. Check the quality of the transfer by lifting up the tracing every once in a while. After the entire design is transferred, remove the transfer paper and tracing paper.

MASKING: LEAF MOTIF

3 Load a no. 4 round brush with masking fluid and begin carefully painting inside the design lines. You want to achieve full coverage inside the design lines. The masking fluid will protect the design. Let the fluid dry to a clear state.

4 Brush on a Metallic Gold glaze over the entire surface with a glaze application brush. Create a strie finish in the background by dragging the flogger brush from one end of the surface to the other. Keep consistent pressure and a straight direction with the brush.

5 After the gold glaze is thoroughly dry, you can remove the masking. Rub the edge of the masked area with your finger to get it started pulling off the surface. It's a "rubbery" substance that will pull off fairly easily. Rub your hand over the surface to make sure all dried masking fluid has been removed.

6 To define the leaf motif, outline and create some interior lines (veins) with gold glaze loaded on a no. 1 script liner brush. Use a light touch on the brush to execute fine, consistent line work. Thin the glaze with water if it does not flow off your brush's tip. Trim the edges in gold foil.

TOLE PAINTING: PENNSYLVANIA DUTCH

Photo of detail on Pennsylvania Dutch tole-painted box.

The graphic stroke work and bright colors of the Pennsylvania Dutch artwork attracts the eye like a magnet. One of the most well known Pennsylvania Dutch symbols is the hex sign design. Tole painting, originally completed on tin or metalware, is now painted on a variety of surfaces. This box design draws on these two traditions. Due to its simplicity, this style creates a very pleasing experience for the viewer. A distressed wood look provides the right backdrop for the design work on top. The painted design was antiqued in a black glaze to create additional patina. ⤫

TOOLS AND MATERIALS

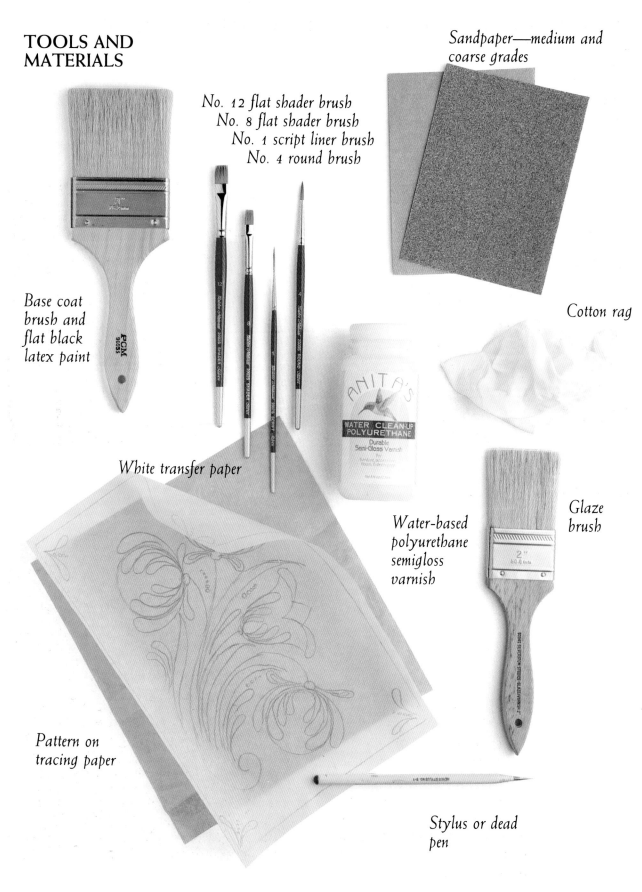

Sandpaper—medium and coarse grades

No. 12 flat shader brush
No. 8 flat shader brush
No. 1 script liner brush
No. 4 round brush

Base coat brush and flat black latex paint

Cotton rag

White transfer paper

Water-based polyurethane semigloss varnish

Glaze brush

Pattern on tracing paper

Stylus or dead pen

COLOR CHIPS—ARTIST'S ACRYLICS AND WATER-BASED GLAZES

Alizarin Crimson
Bright red
Cadmium Red Light
Cadmium Yellow
    Medium

Ultramarine Blue
White plus
    Ultramarine
    Blue plus black
Phthalo Green plus
    black
Phthalo Green

Burnt Umber plus
    Alizarin
    Crimson
Burnt Umber
Dark brown glaze
Indian Brown glaze

Mars Black
Titanium White

1 Using an unfinished box, stain the raw wood with a combination of dark brown plus Indian Brown. Rub on the glaze with a cotton rag and let it dry. Base coat the box with a flat black latex with the base coat bristle brush. Apply several coats and let dry. Distress the surface by sanding with coarse and medium-grade sandpaper to expose the stained layer below.

2 Base the leaflike shapes in Phthalo Green plus black plus a little Cadmium Yellow Medium (a leaf-green tone). Stroke on leaves with a combination of comma strokes and S strokes using a no. 4 round brush. Base the ball flowers in bright red, using a no. 12 flat for the center and the round brush for the side comma-stroke petals. Re-coat until opaque.

3 With the round brush, overstroke the ball flowers with Cadmium Red Light strokes on the right side and Burnt Umber plus Alizarin Crimson on the left side. Base the tulip in a light blue mixture of white plus Ultramarine Blue plus black using the no. 8 flat brush. Overstroke the leaves with another coat of green mixture.

4 Re-stroke the light and dark comma strokes on the red ball flowers using the round brush. Over-stroke the tulip flower in a mixture of a darker blue (light blue plus more Ultramarine Blue and black), making a series of comma strokes. Add a small amount of light blue to white and paint a few comma strokes on the tulip.

5 Overstroke the leaf shapes with Cadmium Yellow Medium, exe-cuting comma and S strokes within the green strokes. Add a series of de-scending red dots in a few places and sign your name with the script liner brush. Let the painting dry thor-oughly, and then place a coat of var-nish over the surface. Let it dry. Brush on a black or brown glaze over the painting and wipe away the excess.

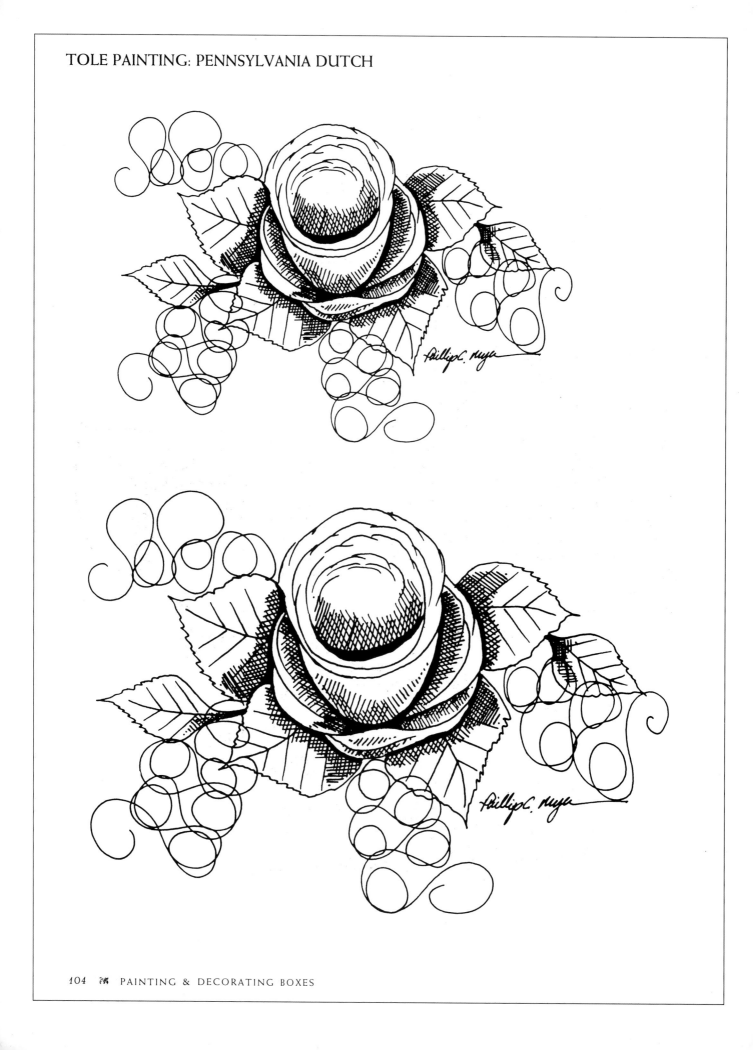

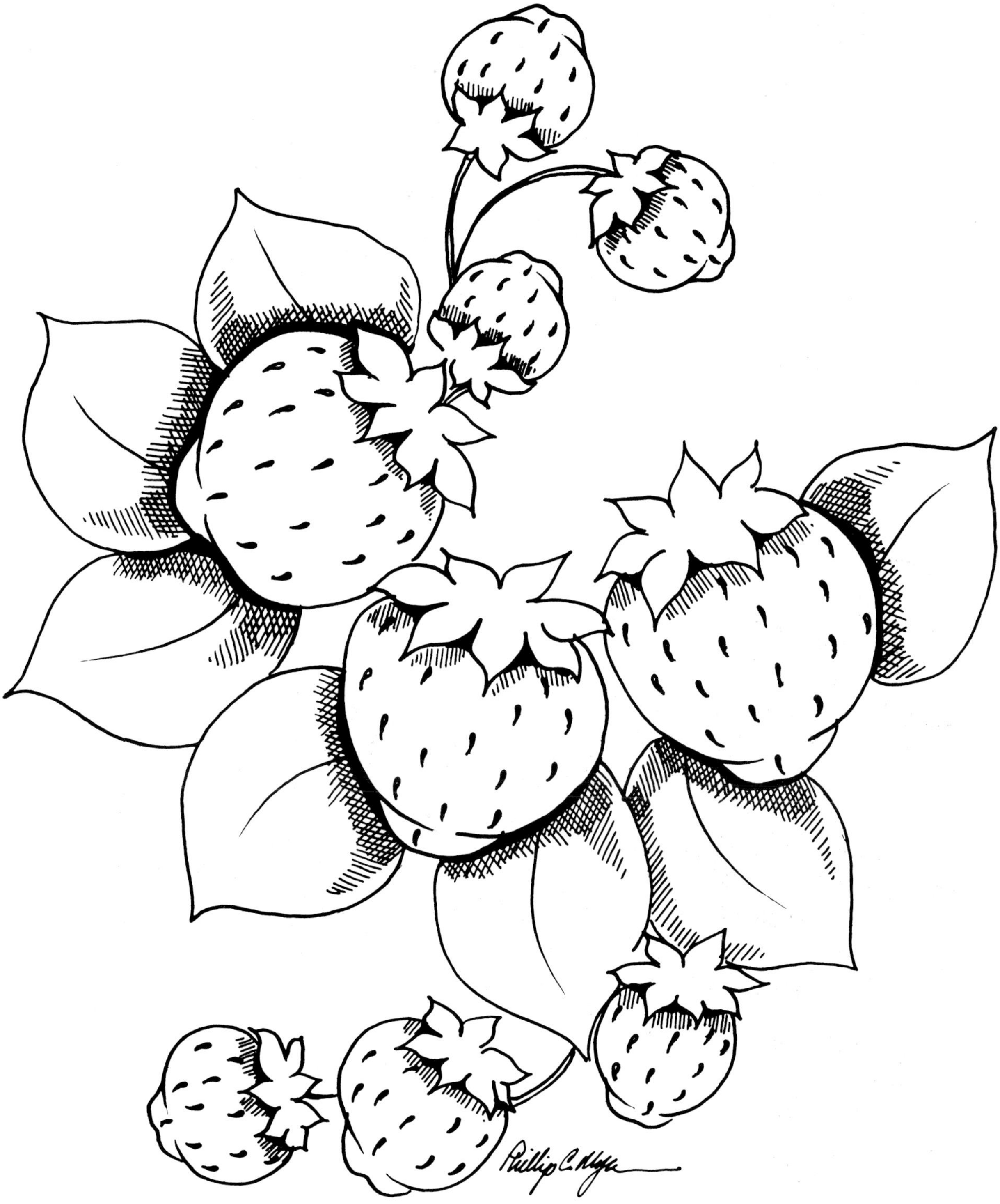

GLOSSARY

ACRYLIC POLYMER—a thermoplastic resin with a synthetic substance or mixture, used as a binder with powdered pigments in the creation of artist's acrylic colors.

ANTIQUING—the application of a very thin, transparent coating over a surface to provide the illusion of age and patina.

ARTIST'S ACRYLIC COLORS—paint that is a mixture of powdered pigments ground in thermoplastic, synthetic emulsions. They can be thinned and cleaned up with water.

BASE COAT—the initial application of paint to a surface.

BODY—the weight or form of an object; as it relates to paint, the consistency can carry a form or volume.

BURNISH—to polish, or to rub a surface with a hard tool, especially to adhere and smooth areas.

CHISEL—the sharp edge that forms on the end of a well-crafted flat brush.

COLOR VALUES—the degrees of lightness, darkness, saturation and brightness of a hue.

CRACKLED—when a surface shows random separations in its paint or varnish finish, making it appear older than it really is; it can result from product incompatibility, temperature or weather.

CRISSCROSS—a paint stroke direction that forms crossed lines, overlapping randomly, making X shapes.

CURTAINING—the sagging or dripping of a layer of paint or varnish that has been placed over a previous coat that is not cured and dried; the top layer weights down the first layer that is not dried and pulls both layers down like sagging "curtain."

DARK VALUE—the deeper color tones on the gray scale that can be created from any color by the addition of black or its color complement.

DECORATIVE PAINTING—an ornamental art form used to decorate functional as well as nonfunctional surfaces; it is a teachable art form broken down into step-by-step methods.

DECOUPAGE—the French art form of cutting and pasting down images to form decorative treatments on a surface.

DISTRESSING—the action of battering a surface with abrasive tools such as sandpaper, hammer, nail, screw or chains; the goal is to imitate age and the wear and tear of a surface.

DOUBLE LOAD—to carry two colors on a brush at one time, side by side, with a smooth color gradation between them.

EARTH TONES—colors that are made with natural pigments (such as Yellow Ochre, which is made from refined clay).

FAUX—the French word which translates as "false" or "fake"; as it relates to painted finishes, it defines a painted look that mimics a real surface: *faux* marble—painted to look like marble, *faux* bois—painted to look like wood grain.

FLAT—as it relates to paint, the sheen or finish that is dull and porous.

FLECKS—small particles of paint spattered on the surface.

FLYSPECKING—the painting technique that disperses small particles of paint over the surface using a toothbrush and thin-consistency paint.

FREEHAND—to create without the use of patterns or guidelines.

FOIL GILDING—an inexpensive and quick technique using foil to achieve a look similar to traditional gilding with real or imitation metal leaf.

GLAZE—a transparent mixture of color plus a clear painting medium.

GLOSS—the highest level of a finish's sheen or shine qualities.

GRAY SCALE—a standardized chart of values from white to black (from lightest to darkest) in percentage increments.

GRID—a framed structure of equally spaced parallel and crossbars used to paint various tile or stripe patterns. A grid is also used to enlarge or reduce the size of designs by scaling them up or down proportionately.

HAZE—a transparent but cloudy or smoky coating over a surface that obstructs the clarity of the color below.

HIGH CONTRAST—an extreme color value difference in close proximity; the highest level would be from white to gray to black in a short distance.

HUE—the quality of color; the intensity of color, as in a shade or tint.

INKLIKE CONSISTENCY—paint thinned with painting medium, painting glaze or solvent to the liquid state that matches drawing ink.

LATEX—paint made from powdered pigments ground with emulsion of rubber or plastic globules. It can be cleaned with water.

LIFT OFF—the intentional or accidental removal of base coat, paint finish or varnish.

LIGHT VALUE—the brighter color values on the gray scale. Any color can become a light value by the addition of white.

MARBLEIZING—the act of reproducing a marble pattern through the use of paint, applied with a brush and/or feathers on a surface.

MASKING—to mark off an area and then protect that area by covering with tape or other items so that it won't receive paint when a nearby area is being painted.

MEDIUM—the type of paint used, such as acrylics or oils; or a liquid, such as water-based varnish, acrylic retarder or water, used to thin acrylic paints.

MEDIUM VALUE—a color tone that is, simply, not too dark and not too light; a shade in the middle from dark value to light value.

MIDTONE—a center point of a color's value in relation to its lightest or darkest points within a given painted area.

MONTAGE—to overlap design elements on a surface until very little or nothing of the original surface shows; a technique employed in decoupage.

MULTITONE—the development of a variety of values of one color or many colors on a surface.

OPAQUE—paint coverage thick enough that light cannot pass through it.

OPEN TIME—the period in which the paints, painting mediums or varnishes will remain workable before they begin to set up and dry.

PAINT RUNS—usually undesirable drips of paint or varnish that move down a vertical surface.

PASTE WAX—a coating of specially designed wax that is rubbed on and adds a level of polish and sheen to a surface.

PATINA—the marks and signs of age that develop on a surface and create character; the corrosion that occurs as metals oxidize.

PATTERN—a guideline to follow when creating, as in woodworking, sewing or decorative painting.

POROUS—a surface that has openings through which moisture easily penetrates.

PRIMER—an opaque, paintlike base coat application that seals the surface and readies it for decorative treatment; a stain-blocking sealer that does not allow bottom coats to penetrate through.

RETARDER—an agent that suspends and slows down the quick drying time of some water-based products, such as acrylics.

RULING—painted trim work of fine lines made through the application of thin-consistency paint with a ruling pen.

SAGGING—the lifting and dropping of a coat of paint due to improper surface preparation.

SATIN—a step up from a flat finish; a surface with a slight amount of sheen or shine.

SEMIGLOSS—a surface with a sheen level greater than satin but less than gloss.

SETUP TIME—the period it takes for paint, painting glaze or varnish to begin to dry and become tacky.

SIDE LOAD—to carry color only on one side of the brush with painting medium or solvent on the other, creating a blended transition on the brush from opaque color to transparent color to no color.

SOLVENT—the agent that cleans and thins such materials as paint, varnishes and painting mediums. A paint's solvent can be used as a painting medium; the solvent for acrylic is water, the solvent for oils is turpentine.

SPACKLING COMPOUND—also called plaster patch, it is a thick-bodied, plasterlike substance that is used to fill in holes.

SPONGING—the painted-finish techniques that use the application of paint loaded on a sponge to create a textural pattern on a surface.

STENCIL—a sheet of Mylar, acetate or heavy card stock with a design cut into it.

STENCILING—the decorative application of design work achieved by brushing or spraying paint through a cut design opening.

STRIE—the painted-finish technique that creates irregular linear streaks in a wet paint glaze through the use of a flogger brush.

STRIPING—the addition of horizontal or vertical lines (or a combination of both) in any degree of line width.

STRIPPING—the removal of paint, varnish or other buildup on a surface through the use of commercially made chemical products and scraping tools.

TACKY—a sticky quality that develops during the drying time of a paint product. Some techniques require waiting for a tacky paint/glue/varnish state before proceeding with the technique.

TELEGRAPHING—the action of an impression or pattern coming up from a foundation level and exposing itself through the top layers that were placed over it.

THICK, CREAMY CONSISTENCY—a paint mixed with a very small amount of painting medium, paint glaze or solvent, whipped to the texture of whipped butter; paint should hold peaks when patted with palette knife.

THIN, CREAMY CONSISTENCY—a paint mixed with painting medium, paint glaze or solvent to the texture of whipped cream.

THIN, SOUPY CONSISTENCY—a paint mixed with painting medium, paint

glaze or solvent to the texture of
watered-down soup.

TONAL & GRADATION—the creation
of various color tones that intermingle and go down the gray scale in an
even transition.

TONE ON TONE—the layering of subtle color values very close in lightness
or darkness on the gray scale.

TRANSPARENT—a coating of paint or
glaze so thin that light can easily pass
through; when something is transparent, you can see through it clearly.

VALUE—the ratio or percentage of
color that relates to the gray scale;
a color from lightest to darkest.

VARNISH—a clear coating of either
a polyurethane water-based or oil-based product that protects what is
underneath the coating.

VEINS—the interior pattern element
found in leaf structures as well as marble surfaces.

WASH—paint that is thinned with
enough painting medium, paint glaze
or solvent to make it fluid and
transparent.

WET SANDING—the smoothing of
a surface with a fine, wet/dry sand-paper, wet with water and soap. This
application is completed in the finishing stage, removing any imperfections between coats of varnish.

WOOD GRAIN—the pattern of marks
found in wood surfaces; a flowing organic pattern.

WOOD GRAINING—the painted finish
that duplicates a wood type through
the use of a wet paint glaze, brushes
and tools.

WOOD PUTTY—the thick compound
made of whiting, linseed oil and binders in a doughlike consistency, used
to fill imperfections on a wood surface before painting or finishing.

SOURCES

*T*he following companies are the manufacturers, mail order suppliers or facilities which offer instructional materials or seminars that may be of interest to you. Please write for further information. Many times, a self-stamped, self-addressed return envelope will provide you with a response.

Below are resources for the specific materials used in the creation of the decorated boxes in this book:

BRUSHES
Silver Brush Limited
92 N. Main St., Bldg. 18C
Windsor, NJ 08561
(609) 443-4900 Phone
(609) 443-4888 Fax

GLAZES, GLUES, DESIGN PRESSES & VARNISHES
Back Street, Inc.
3905 Steve Reynolds Blvd.
Norcross, GA 30093
(770) 381-7373 Phone
(770) 381-6424 Fax

PAINTS—ARTIST'S ACRYLICS
Martin/F. Weber Co.
2727 Southampton Rd.
Philadelphia, PA 19154
(215) 677-5600 Phone
(215) 677-3336 Fax

TAPES
3M Consumer Products Group
P.O. Box 33053
St. Paul, MN 55133
(612) 733-1110 Phone

UNFINISHED BOXES
The following companies produce the unfinished boxes decorated in this book:

- Woodgraining:
  Bird's Eye Maple Box
- Tin Piercing:
  Graphic Design Box
- Crackling:Foil Finish Box
- Woodgraining: Mahogany Box
- Masking: Leaf Motif Box

ArtCraft Wood Etc.
415 E. Seventh St.
Joplin, MO 64801
(417) 782-7063 Phone
(417) 782-7064 Fax

- Fabric Covering: Ivy Print Box

Back Street, Inc.
3905 Steve Reynolds Blvd.
Norcross, GA 30093
(770) 381-7373 Phone
(770) 381-6424 Fax

- Stamping: Celestial Design Box
- Dimensional Decorative
  Painting: Strawberry Box
- Paper Covering:
  Marbleized and Natural Box

- Lace Stenciling:
  Rose and Leaf Box

Decorator & Craft Corporation

428 S. Zelta
Wichita, KS 67207
(316) 685-6265 Phone
(316) 685-7606 Fax

- Stone Finishing:
  Lapis Lazuli Box

Italian Touch

2416 Calle Soria
Santa Barbara, CA 93109
(805) 965-5448 Phone
(805) 965-8712 Fax

- Decoupage: Fruit Design Box
- Tole Painting:
  Pennsylvania Dutch Box

Two Day Designs

Route 1, Box 162-A
Eastanollee, GA 30538
(706) 779-5485 Phone
(706) 779-5485 Fax

- Marbleizing: Green Fantasy Box
- Design Pressing: Vegetable Box

Walnut Hollow

Route 1
Dodgeville, WI 53533
(608) 935-2341 Phone
(608) 935-3029 Fax

SCHOOLS

The following are schools that specialize in the teaching of paint and *faux* finishes for the decoration of accessories, furniture and interiors:

American Academy of Decorative Finishes

14255 N. Seventy-Ninth St., Suite 10
Scottsdale, AZ 85260
(602) 991-8560 Phone
(602) 991-9779 Fax

Day Studio Workshop, Inc.

1504 Bryant St.
San Francisco, CA 94103
(415) 626-9300 Phone

Finishing School, Inc.

334 Main St.
Port Washington, NY 11050
(516) 767-6422 Phone
(516) 767-7406 Fax

PCM Studios

School of the Decorative Arts
731 Highland Ave. NE, Suite D
Atlanta, GA 30312
(404) 222-0348 Phone
(404) 222-0348 Fax

Students at PCM Studios learning paint and faux *finishes.*

INDEX